The Happiness Lie

al-che-my

1: seemingly magical power or process of transmuting

2: an ancient practice focused on changing base metals into gold

3: an analogy for human transformation

What People Are Saying

(Comments left on Cindy's website after client sessions, typo's corrected.)

What a GIFT, what a GIFT! I had no idea what to expect with the phone session but am now feeling love, joy, and happiness and some tears of JOY. It was like sharing with my best friend, some personal grief issues, which quickly disappeared with a few short questions to my body. It was a magical experience. ~ Wilda Hicks

I learned more today, in our first session, than I have in all the years I have been around. ~ Peg Jones

Although we initially called about our daughter, Cindy helped us realize the importance of not just holding the space for her, but ultimately taking responsibility for only our OWN selves. Full of gratitude ~ Veronica and Zeke Rios, USA

I've been searching for a way out of my old patterns of fear and pain and sadness. I'm looking forward to putting this new shift in attention/awareness into action. Thank you, Cindy, for so generously giving of your time and your spirit. Namaste. ~ Kathryn

It was an amazing experience to share/play with someone who knows the territory of who we truly are so intimately. I especially appreciated the notion of practicing being happy for no reason. It is so liberating to know that there is a whole different way of living within the world than the one we were "programmed" to believe was the truth. Now things are opening in an exponential way, and I find myself being highly amused by what used to cause me intense suffering. I laugh a lot more. The world is bright and full of magic. Life is much more fun. ~ Leslie Titcombe, PQ

This session felt "heavenly" and there simply are no words to describe it. I can now celebrate not only who I am but also who others are, and this is what makes me very happy. I am back to being present, feeling joyful and ecstatic. This truly is *Alchemy* ~ Christine xox

I felt like I was talking to a long lost friend, and Cindy made so many things clearer for me. I loved how she would catch me and show me by using questions how to see the truth in every experience. *The Alchemy of Love and Joy* is going to help so many people. I would highly recommend people book a session with you and of course BUY THE BOOK. Thank you for sharing your JOY. ~ Sharon

It is wondrous how quickly my experience changed from feeling sad, hopeless, discouraged and lost to incredible peace, presence, calm and a quiet joy that is expanding as I now speak about it. This is a magical switch! This practice has literally switched the track I was on. Doing this practice revealed how my negative beliefs were just negative thoughts I believed!! But they were just thoughts and they could be dropped!!! And in dropping them, their power instantly dissolved, and so did my sadness. In fact I laughed because the relief was so easy, and also at the illusion of how truly unfounded were the thoughts that I was so fervently believing! This practice is indeed *Alchemy*—it transformed my experience in my body, mind, and especially my heart. Thank you Cindy for so generously sharing your insight. The truth really does set us free and how great to travel there on the wings of joy!!! ~ Nicole, Ottawa, ON

Cindy has an intuitive ability to change your perspective. I loved the way I "flipped" into the feeling of "I have." ~ Lynda, Saskatchewan

I feel that finding Cindy and discovering her simple teachings has been a magical experience leading me to a transformation to my most natural way of being. The word *Alchemy* is so fitting. I now have a simple formula for changing the way I feel, the way I live, and my whole way of being. I have been released from believing the thoughts that enter my consciousness that make me feel bad. I realize that I have the power to choose what I put my attention on. I know that when I feel good I have a greater capacity to share who I truly am with the world – a loving human being. ~ Anna, Ottawa, ON

How does respect and appreciation feel? Cindy won't tell you how it feels to feel good, she holds a space and opening for you to experience it. Through her simple process of looking, recognizing, breathing, discarding and – being – WOW! I'm sure each *Alchemy* session is as unique as every individual, but it left me lighter, more apt to deal compassionately with difficult situations and my time spent with Cindy allowed me to relax, laugh, and feel. Like a gold mine in this age of economy based on information and exchange, Cindy enables people to be rich! Namaste ~ Natalie

Cindy's technique is very practical, relevant and tailored specifically for you. Once you tap into the feeling that you want to have in that instance, you then magnify it – so that your actions, and hence life, are progressive. I really enjoyed my session with Cindy. ~ Andrew Flanagan

"The onus is on the Universe" was my epiphany when working with Cindy. Thank you, Cindy, for helping me experience this clarity and sharing in the energy and laughter that followed! Blessings of universal abundance to all! ~ Kim, Ottawa, ON

Cindy gave all her transformational talent and energy to guiding me through a very substantive shift. Re-sorting, I've been through a number of other modalities for these kinds of shifts and I find Cindy's process to be extremely effective in creating real change. ~ Joanne Sprott

I had this knowledge that I tend to live in my head. Using yoga, reiki, and meditation, I have had glimpses of how being present in the moment feels—but none so powerful as the time with Cindy this morning. I could truly feel the difference between being constricted by my thoughts and the expansiveness of being joyfully in my body. It is amazing to think we have this power and the ability to easily access and sustain it. I look forward to continuing to grow, share, and practice this blessed gift. ~ Lisa Walls

"We don't want things or people—we want the feeling we mistake them for." There was an aha moment when I understood these wise words of yours. I fell into how it would feel to have what I wanted. I accessed it and yet nothing had changed in my world other than allowing myself to have it. I have the power! Thank you Cindy for your spiritual wisdom, for the simplicity and practicality of your wonderful technique, for your generosity, and for your God-filled laughter. ~ Katherine

Cindy's technique is very practical and tailored specifically for you and your life. She will work with you on a particular instance from your own life, and let you experience the joy available to you in that instance. Cindy can show you how a "feelingization" can change your perspective entirely, and simply, bring you joy. Who doesn't need more of that? ~ Linda

Published by Go Beyond
www.GoBeyond.ca

Teevens, Cindy
The Happiness Lie
What Generations Have Been Told
That Makes You Unhappy

Editor: Karah Madrone, http://WordStrengthEditing.com
Cover design: N. G. Panetta, npanetta@mail.com

Copies are available in quantity discounts when used to
promote select products or services, or for use in study groups
or for educational purposes by associations. For information or
to apply, contact the publisher: info@gobeyond.ca

ISBN: 978-0-9813763-2-5

Body - Mind - Spirit
1. Happiness 2. Self-Help 3. Spirituality

The Happiness Lie

What Generations Have Been Told That Makes You Unhappy

U.S. NATIONAL CRISIS HOT LINES

Suicide Line
1-800-784-2433

Talk Line
1-800-273-8255

Deaf Hotline
1-800-799-4TTY (4889)

or in an emergency dial 911

CANADIAN NATIONAL CRISIS HOT LINES

Crisis Line
1-866-996-0991

Kids Help Phone
1-800-668-6868

Deaf Hot Line (TDD)
1-800-567-5803

or in an emergency dial 911

There are also specific crisis lines for problems like child or elder abuse, drugs, alcohol, domestic violence, cancer, aids, rape, depression, etc. You can search the internet for a crisis line for your specific needs or call one of the above.

Acknowledgments

Years of working with hundreds of people captured and honed the information in this book. My clients have taught me so much about how to succinctly and powerfully express what needs expressing; what aids them the most in personal breakthroughs. This book is the co-creative result of all of your time, effort, and desire for freedom and inner peace and happiness. This is your book.

Thank-you, N.G.; your original, creative representation of society's perilous condition on the cover is pure talent. Pinocchio's self-inflicted existence, trapped by lies, with strings that could be pulled by others—and the belief that this is happiness, could not be more vividly portrayed.

Deep gratitude goes to Karah Madrone, my editor, for not compromising, for persisting in pulling out of me full explanations that create clear expression and aid understanding. Your keen knowledge of *Alchemy*, skill in seeing, and talent in writing has brought this book to the next level for the reader.

Contents

Prologue

What if everything you thought you knew about happiness was *wrong?*

When would you want to know?

The danger of not knowing is a potential lifetime of mental, emotional, and physical stress and suffering.

The Gain of Pain

Mental-emotional stress triggers physical issues:
- high blood pressure, sleepless nights, headaches
- mental-emotional anguish, illness
- over-eating, under-eating, and
- abuse of alcohol or drugs.

Stress and suffering do relationship damage by:
- blocking your clarity,
- interfering with your ability to hear what the other is actually saying, and
- stirring fear, anger, and judgmental thinking that when acted upon, can destroy a relationship.

It can career your career by:
- affecting your ability to work with and positively interact with co-workers and bosses, or
- stifling your creativity and problem-solving power.

Your wallet is not left alone either, potentially
- draining resources due to poor judgment, overspending,
- spontaneous emotional buying, and lack of planning. This could all add up to
- debt, and you might even
- avoid the mail and bills, compounding your problems.

We are paying the high price of stress in personal cost, billions of dollars lost in business, stress-related illness, depression, medication, and suicide rates that are at all-time highs[1]. Children are not even immune anymore; child depression drug use has quadrupled in a decade[1]. Just what is going on here?

Our Society Has Been Put on a Futile Path

We've been collecting more and more things, people, events, and experiences but it has not made us happier - in fact that pursuit has made us miserable, and for some, even depressed or suicidal.

This realization is important for all people, whether worry and fear wakes you up at night or keeps you on edge during the day, whether you are struggling with bad thoughts and feelings or depression, or whether you just don't know the truth about what actually causes your pain or happiness. Until the lie is exposed, and the truth known, we will keep each other and the next generation functioning in the same dysfunctional way.

The Loss of Joy

Not only do we maximize our pain, but we limit our love, joy, and inner peace. Beyond the pain and cost of stress and suffering, what if you are capable of a joy and bliss beyond belief, and you don't even know it?

What could you gain? What would be the lifetime cost of that loss? Minimally, wouldn't you be curious to discover it?

I was shocked at how easy it was to feel good, and at how much I had been missing; deep peace, fearless freedom, and access to love and connection whenever and wherever I want it.

Sound good? Wait, it gets better, because the discovery doesn't cost anything and it takes no additional time or effort because it's about how you are being, not what you are doing.

(1) Visit http://InnerAlcove.com/statistics

Chapter 1

The Fairytale Girl

Once upon a time, there lived a little girl who was originally full of wonder at the world and curiously asked questions like, "How did I get here? What am I doing here? Where did I come from? Where do I go from here?" But her questions fell on deaf ears, partly, she realized, because people don't know, and partly because they were afraid and didn't want to know, or were perhaps embarrassed that they didn't know.

So while almost all of her other questions were answered, this line of questioning was shunned and suppressed with admonishments like, "Don't ask that question," "That's a silly question," "Stop thinking so much," "Just get on with your life." The message received was: Nobody else asks those questions, so just do what everybody else does.

With no hope of answers coming from anywhere, she gave up, partly due to the realization that nobody could or would answer them, and partly due to the already implanted need to feel okay, to feel normal based on the acceptance of others. Now, normal is not necessarily healthy or truthful—it's just common. Yes, over time, she was partly assimilated into the unconsciousness of the masses. I say partly because while the questions may have been suppressed, they never left her.

Born in the sixties, like all other kids she was rewarded (or was it bribed?) with candy and toys. They included Santa's promise (or was it a threat?) of withholding gifts on that great day that only came once a year, with the cliché, "Have you been bad or good?"

Like the generation before, mistaking things for happiness, she learned to long (inside) for what she did not have (on the outside).

She fell for fairy tales of great fanfare and importance about others girls who would become unhappy "old maids" if they did not find the perfect partner before thirty. Raised in the seventies and eighties, there was a myriad of songs that she learned to mindlessly repeat, not unlike a mantra: "You are my everything, I can't live without you, you're all I ever needed, you're the one, you're my reason for living, etc.," pretending and projecting that love existed somewhere outside of her.

A lot of these confused songs were also about pain, and so she began to believe the lie that love hurts. She was taught, through countless conscious and unconscious means, through movies, music, family, friends, TV, religion, fear, gossip, marketing, news, magazines, and more that her happiness, love, and peace of mind depended on some "thing," person, or event outside of herself. Before she could even recognize, comprehend, or put into words our innate inner joy, her blissful birthright was mentally buried. That little girl was me.

I say that it was only buried, not destroyed, because later, as an adult, that bliss burst forth again in all its grand glory. There was a lot of pain before that breakthrough, but this revolutionary tale is a true story, and it does have a happy ending.

Persevere with me; if your romantic bubble and treasured beliefs are popped along the way, it can only be because something infinitely greater awaits you.

Chapter 2

How Suicide Led to the Discovery of Joy

A True Tale

You may have identified with that little girl, whatever your gender, because we were all exposed to the same hand-me-down beliefs and conditioning.

My father was no exception, and he suffered severely for extended periods of time, which resulted in suicide. My whole experience through that, which I write more about in my first book, *Alchemy*, launched me on a quest to find an end to suffering. I was driven to find a way to control my state, but in that quest was gifted with so much more.

How I dealt with my own unrelated suffering freed me. But first, let me set the stage. Being raised with the fear of being separated out and identified as "abnormal," we crumble to pressure to conform, and unknowingly adopt other people's beliefs as our own. Having bought into the belief that we need other people's love, which implies that love comes from others and is outside ourselves, I was vulnerable to love being taken away from me. And it happened; I was denied what I thought was my source of love and joy, and felt abandoned, misled, and lied to in the process.

This suffering was nothing special, it was no different from what everyone else has experienced when love is apparently denied. The details are not important because what matters is not the story, nor even the suffering, but this time what I did *differently*–right in the middle of it—and how that changed everything. What was possible for me, is possible for all.

Looking for understanding, meaning, something to grasp onto, something to accept, while not accepting what had happened, and also seeking relief, I noticed that I was the one who felt pain with absolutely every judgmental "staining" thought that arose about another. So I rejected them all. To tarnish someone creates separation and pain. I did not want that for myself or anyone; I wanted only unconditional love, all round.

Giving and having only unconditional love meant to accept others' choices, thoughts, beliefs, and actions with love, even if these apparently affected me negatively. To truly do that, I had to have zero tolerance for blaming anything or anyone outside of me for how I felt. These choices—no, these decisions— forced me to take one-hundred-percent responsibility for what I felt, forced me to find the truth about the cause of what I felt, and forced me to detach from needing the outside. Since blaming, which was my usual way out of a painful experience up until then, was no longer an option, I went inside, deeply inside.

There were intense weeks of pain and suffering. I had put myself in a box with no known way out. My mind whirled like a tornado. I did not want things to be as they were, but they were as they were. Thoughts like "How could this be?" and "This should not be," fueled the funnel to spin faster and higher. Everything tossed in was shattered into shards that ripped and tore me up inside. "I want" was the deadliest, most painful, and most futile thought, yet it was also the one that pointed out the reality that, in fact, I did not have what I wanted and no matter how badly "I wanted" in my mind, no matter how much I suffered in that moment, facts were not going to change.

Trapped by desperately seeking relief while simultaneously wanting to give love no matter what, I came to an end and the box exploded. For me, suffering was no longer an option, just like blaming was no longer an option. I clearly saw that suffering does not change anything, and for a brief moment, not knowing what else to do, I just stopped.

In this fleeting moment of stillness I knew or remembered or heard, "You can give yourself whatever you want." Then the mental-emotional pain began to build again and in the middle of intense suffering, I wondered, "Well, even if that were true, what do I want?"

At the time, there were a lot of things I wanted: acceptance, connection, dignity and respect, and mostly love, true love. If you can give yourself what you want, then it does not come from the outside; so I pulled my attention from the outside. Then it happened.

Instead of putting my attention on what I didn't want and what I didn't have on the outside, I went inside and looked for everything I did want—and there they were! All of the intense energy that was being used to feel bad instantly flipped over into feeling good. Then it flipped back. But I had caught a glimpse—whoa!—*what was that?*

Again, I looked within for what I did want, and once again it was all there! In the middle of unwanted outside circumstances, in the middle of my suffering, I found immediate joy: a complete and radical reversal of feeling in the moment. Instantly, happiness blossomed and immense pleasure began to fill my body from everywhere, all at once. Seeking the acceptance I wanted, it was there, as was the connection, respect, dignity, and even love. One by one, I recognized them all and basked in ever-expanding happiness, peace, and joy. This was so simple, yet radically powerful!

At first it seemed hard to believe, yet there it was: joy. Then I thought perhaps it wouldn't last, but it was such a relief that I kept my attention on the good feeling. My actual experience went against my beliefs at the time, so I thought that maybe this reversal could not be repeated. But I had been hurting so much for so long, and I wanted to feel good more than I wanted the outside to change (and it wasn't changing, anyway), so I clung to the joy, and it stayed, repeated, and settled in.

What I have come to call "old-mind" did battle with me for a few weeks and habitual thoughts arose like, "But you can't feel good because A, B, C, has happened," and you certainly can't feel joyful!" Yet in spite of my circumstances, I did. "But I AM feeling it!" was the indisputable answer. Having discovered this inner joy, I put my attention on it and ignored thoughts about the outside.

We cannot experience something that we think is impossible; we simply must be congruent. One or the other, the experience or the belief, has to go. Having suffered so long, I was not about to let the joy go. Experiencing joy while knowing the facts destroyed my belief that I had to feel bad, and feeling good became my highest priority.

At times there was flip-flopping between automatic, habitual suffering and feeling good, but I persisted in seeking good feeling, again and again. When a bad feeling was noticed, I would seek what was wanted; I would seek the opposite. I would seek joy. "Seeing" the suffering arise and causing joy right in the middle of it, made me spontaneously burst out laughing. That experience was as funny as seeing the powerlessness of the outside world to affect me inside.

The happiness and gratitude that grew within could not be contained. I was compelled to write my first book, *Alchemy,*

How To Feel Good No Matter What, and to speak with people, showing them how to shift their state.

The feeling that love has been lost or taken away is one of the most excruciating experiences (and the stuff of many famous painful love songs). This makes sense, because love is your very essence. Yet the truth and reality is that you can't lose your essence.

While you can't lose love, you can have the feeling of "lost love," which is the opposite feeling of love. Still, love *itself* does not hurt. We can only ever feel one or the other at a time: love or lost love. Love is always there and available; it's just not being known. It's not being known because it is believed to be lost.

Your imagined "object" of love may have left your life, but love can only be objectified in the mind, not in reality. It is still eternally available to you. The poet Rumi said it best: "While you go looking for trinkets, your treasure house awaits you in your own being."

Having lived with your current elevated level of pain and diminished joy for so long, you may not know the true extent of either in your life, nor their potential.

So the first step is to discover what your happiness ratio is.

Chapter 3

What is Your Happiness Ratio?

To discover how much stress or happiness you are experiencing, and how free you are, take the quiz below and evaluate your happiness ratio.

1) Check-off "Yes" to the statements that apply to you. In each case, only check yes if you are fully in agreement and believe this to be true for you. (e.g. If you realize that "sometimes I feel inferior" then you cannot answer "Yes" that you feel "equal to everyone" in B-10, for if you are equal to every one, you are equal all the time.)

2) Base your answers on how you are actually living and experiencing life, not on what your ideals are.

3) In order for this to help and be of use, you must be honest with yourself.

PART A) Do you:

- ☐ Worry about the future?
- ☐ Think about the past, wish you could change it, or think "If only I had..."?
- ☐ Feel that you aren't smart enough?
- ☐ Believe that other people can drag you down?
- ☐ Believe that something is wrong with your life?
- ☐ Blame yourself for things you did?
- ☐ Feel inferior or judge yourself?
- ☐ Tell others about bad things that happened to you?
- ☐ Don't feel that you deserve what you want?
- ☐ Struggle with life?
- ☐ Think that there is something wrong with others?
- ☐ Get angry and frustrated often?
- ☐ Call yourself names, or insult yourself?
- ☐ Feel tiny or insignificant?
- ☐ Believe you know what other people think or feel?
- ☐ Hate Mondays or other days of the week?
- ☐ Often need a TV, radio or some sound on?
- ☐ Try to control your thoughts?
- ☐ Feel unappreciated by people around you?
- ☐ Think the world is going downhill?
- ☐ Think you don't have enough money?
- ☐ Dislike being alone, or dislike having company?
- ☐ Feel that others stress you?
- ☐ Feel like you have to change things/people?
- ☐ Lay awake thinking, unable to sleep?
- ☐ Say things you later regret?
- ☐ Analyze your thoughts?
- ☐ Find that people treat you badly?
- ☐ Have needs in relationships?
- ☐ Get involved in conflict easily or often?

_____ Add up your total

PART B) Do you:

- [ ] Experience contentedness?
- [ ] Feel happy no matter the weather?
- [ ] Look forward to the future?
- [ ] Give loving interaction when you want attention?
- [ ] Meditate in silence?
- [ ] Ask politely for what you want?
- [ ] Stay with the present moment?
- [ ] Enjoy every day of the week?
- [ ] Know your thoughts are your friends?
- [ ] Feel equal to anyone and everyone?
- [ ] Feel happy with your circumstances?
- [ ] Know that no one can drag you down?
- [ ] Accept yourself, feel good in your skin?
- [ ] Go with the flow of life?
- [ ] Have no interest in figuring others out?
- [ ] Feel worthy?
- [ ] Live peacefully?
- [ ] Walk or sit with someone without needing to talk?
- [ ] Think the world is a wonderful place?
- [ ] Enjoy being alone?
- [ ] Love without expectation or need?
- [ ] Let things happen rather than make them happen?
- [ ] Sleep well?
- [ ] Not engage in conflict?
- [ ] Have frequent smile attacks?
- [ ] Enjoy all tasks, even "menial" ones?
- [ ] Feel connected to everything, or not separate?
- [ ] Not worry?
- [ ] Experience spontaneous, uncaused outbursts of gratitude or joy?
- [ ] Enjoy quiet time often?

_____ Add up your total

Happiness Ratio Evaluation
Look for the closest match to your ratio:

30 – 0   Extreme suffering. Reach out for help to begin feeling better as you start reconsidering all that you think you know to be true.

20 – 10   Heavy stress. Deep belief in the happiness lie.

15 – 15   Torn. You may be confused with conflicting ideas, and experience ups and downs. Strong belief in the happiness lie, yet beginning to break through. (Also applies if your figures are high or low on both sides; being fairly equal is the tip-off.) You may be highly motivated for change.

10 – 20   Breakthrough. You don't believe much of the happiness lie. You are well on your way, keep going, there are lingering sticking points, and more freedom and a whole lot more joy beyond belief to uncover.

5 – 25   You are so close to freedom. This is quite a physically healthy ratio. You still have remnants of the happiness lie, valuable gems to uncover, and still more joy to unleash and discover.

0 – anything: You are free. You are naturally loving, peaceful, and content. There is no belief in the happiness lie.

If you have even one checkmark on the left, your life could be transformed by putting the material in this book to practice.

The more you live object happiness and tainted attachment love, the higher your left-hand score will be. The more you practice inner happiness and pure love, the higher your right-hand score will be. This book will show you how.

As you can see, the critical side is the left side. The interesting thing is that as you clean-up the left side, the right side simply grows spontaneously.

Get Outer Reflection

Sometimes we can't see the forest for the trees. Please ask for reflection from a close friend or family member before proceeding if your ratio is:

- Either 0-30 or 30-0 (or close to that)
- 0-0 (This ratio should not be, it would mean you are not experiencing either pain or joy at all. So it would have to reflect misunderstanding of how to use the quiz.)

Get someone to look at the questions and your answers, and see if they agree with your ratio. They may offer specific, real life examples that do not agree with your answers. If you agree with the examples they have to offer, modify your score accordingly.

If you think you are always happy and peaceful but family and friends disagree because your outer behavior does not match your inner claim, there is incongruity, which can come from 1) having lived with such high stress for so long that you no longer recognize it. You may not know or experience peace or joy any more, or 2) from a bitter resignation such as, "Oh I don't try to change people because it's a waste of time," attitude. If you are truly stress-free and joyful, your answers should have no trace of bad taste at all, there is only love within, and without, and your behavior reflects that.

It is possible for the happiness quiz answers to be distorted in the mind, so as to give answers that are in no way congruent with the truth of behavior. It is possible for you to calculate a happy-heavy ratio yet actually live a painful existence—that would be a defense mechanism for when there's too much pain. You may think you are being fully honest, but may in fact be numb, unaware, or in denial. Thus, pain may be a constant factor in your life while you refuse to take notice. You may suffer and see others suffer, but not respond.

This may appear to be a most dire situation, but it is also an opportunity in waiting, particularly since you are reading this book. The potential for swift and complete reversal is possible, because nobody wants to hurt, and everybody wants to feel good. You must get honest yet compassionate outer reflection, and allow the light of truth in without blaming yourself or the reflector. With that, you will move on quickly.

Do not discard your whole assessment in favor of another's opinion, just ask if they remember any specific events to offer that may conflict with your answers. If you get an opinion that you are not in agreement with, get additional opinions. If the majority are saying roughly the same thing, you may want to seriously reconsider and look closely at what is actually going on in your life.

While nobody can know your inner truth, if you are honest, sincere, and earnest for joy and freedom then you may want to have someone look at your score regardless of what it is, and at least consider their response.

Start Keeping Track

Write your ratio down on paper and keep it somewhere easy to find, then re-take the quiz some weeks or months after you have been using the practice of *Alchemy*, which you will learn in this book, and compare your figures and findings. It was not until I later saw a similar stress list that I realized just how much I had changed.

The people I have worked with generally report a low left (A) and high right (B) ratio, and when asked what they think their score would have been before we started working together, it's commonly a "flipped" ratio; a complete reversal.

If you checked "think about the past," "worry about the future," or "try to control thoughts," and if you are tired of dredging up the past and working on what seems to be your endless issues, then you are going to love this solution, because it does not involve healing the past or controlling your thoughts.

But first, we need to expose the happiness lie.

Chapter 4

The Happiness Lie

The Elephant in the Room

Young children are born a bundle of joy and we've all seen how they don't need anything from the outside in order to know their inner happiness. They experience pure joy for the sake of joy. They don't need an outside thing, they don't need toys or candy, they don't wait for something "good" to happen, they don't need the approval of others, and they don't need the participation of others. They can switch from crying to giggling, for no reason. They are spontaneous and unlimited. They don't know yet that they "should not" be happy until something considered good by society "makes" them happy.

As a child I understood, "Do what everyone else does," to be a way of saying, "Drop your questions, do this instead and it will make you happy." That command rang repeatedly in my ears, as I saw the plan laid out before me: go to school, get a job, get a car and house, get married, have kids, retire, grow old, and die. What is missing from this picture? I didn't know, but I knew something was missing, so I never fully bought into it. Most people, on some level, don't either.

It is possible, for a while, to live as if the pursuit of material or interpersonal happiness is what this world and life is all about. That pursuit can distract for a time, but the kindness of life is that it keeps pointing to truth. The questions remain unanswered, and there is a nagging inner dissatisfaction.

Like an ugly, ill-fitting, out of style pair of jeans, we've been handed down an ugly lie that does not fit. Out of ignorance, generation after generation has been told that some person, place, thing, or event makes us happy or unhappy. Generation after generation has lived, told, and re-sold the lie to the next generation. Generation after generation has believed it, despite the obvious elephant in the room; despite living with glaring evidence to the contrary.

The Evidence

Have you ever been happy on a sunny day? Have you ever felt bad on a sunny day? Have you ever been happy on a rainy day? Yes, we all have; so what does the weather (or the outside) have to do it? Nothing.

A group of friends got together for a movie one night and two of them were a newly-formed couple. At one point, they snuggled together on the couch. We, of course, all noticed this, and later a friend who was single commented on it, sharing privately that she felt bad. We were both single at the time, but my experience was one of happiness and love. With a closer look, she realized that at first she actually felt good. That was when her attention was on what simply was; two people enjoying affection. Quickly though, and almost unnoticed, her interest and attention went onto "not having that"… and she started to feel bad.

Ultimately she admitted it was not the friends snuggling that caused the pain, it was attention on what she did not want, the thoughts that felt bad, like "I don't have that," "I can't feel love," "I am not as important," "I am not worthy…" It was not the reality or fact of being single that caused her pain—

initially she was perfectly fine, sitting there, single, and even feeling love in the presence of her snuggling friends!

In any given moment, you have the choice of what is most important to you, of what you are most interested in, of what you want to put your attention on and therefore experience.

Have you ever seen a couple kiss in public, and felt good? Have you ever seen a couple kiss in public, and felt bad? Yes, sure, most people have. Situations change. Persons, places, things, or events change, but what is the common denominator? You.

Your pre-existing state or belief, if you are not aware of it, colors your perception and view of things, people, or events—it's not the thing, person, or event that makes you feel that way.

We've been living from the outside in, when life is actually experienced within. Because we think, live, and experience backwards, we feel the need to try to control the outside. We have been set up in a futile pursuit of happiness because we have been looking for happiness where it does not exist.

Things Don't Make You Happy

When you feel happy, where is the feeling? Where does it exist? For example, is it over there in the new car? If it were in the car, you could not feel it. The car would need a bio-body to generate feeling, and even then, it would be the car's feeling, not yours. A car is just two tons of metal, a practical (or impractical) object; there's not one "ounce" of happy in it.

The belief that things, people, or events make us happy has been so ingrained from generation to generation that it is even entrenched in our habitual thought and speech patterns, perhaps to the point that our language itself now contributes to the problem. When I realized the lie, I could no longer speak the way I used to. I'd hear habitual phrases start to come out of my mouth and I'd stop, mid-sentence, as I realized, "*That's not true.*" I had to find different ways of expressing myself in order to stay with integrity and truth. Or I simply dropped thoughts. Now when people say things like, "He hurt me," or "It stresses me," these false imaginings jump out at me like a red flag.

Merely because an idea has been handed down to you and others around you believe it, does not mean it is true. The majority also used to believe that the earth is flat.

Even our physicians and other experts are submerged in the mass unconsciousness, and have contributed to the problem with their prescriptions of, "Do things that make you happy." *Things don't make you happy.* You can walk through a picture-perfect garden or enchanted forest blissfully content or completely miserable, just the same as you can tend to an ailing child either in a state full of love and compassion, or in fear, angst, and suffering. Which is more resourceful? Which do you think would best aid the child?

The Pursuit of Happiness is Futile - Four Proofs

1) The pursuit of happiness makes you unhappy - The "pursuit of happiness" has really been the pursuit of things, people, or events. As long as you believe that things make you happy, then you will also believe that their absence makes you unhappy, and so you engage in stressful chase and worry. True pursuit of happiness would be for freedom *from* things, people, or events.

2) The happiness does not last. If happiness was caused by a thing, person, or event, then once you got what you wanted

you'd be forever happy. But somehow, even before things materially break down, the happiness has already "worn off."

3) The happiness can be lost. If happiness can be given to you in an object, person, or event, then it can be taken away from you. Indeed it *will* be taken from you because nothing in the material world lasts.

4) The pursuit of happiness is a trap. The pursuit of happiness, endlessly chasing one thing after another for a mere moment of happiness, a short respite between dissatisfactions, appears to be freedom, but is actually bondage. Due to ignorance of what is actually going on, one can remain trapped in an infinite cycle of ups and downs.

In summary, the pursuit of happiness is futile because if you don't get what you want, you suffer, and if you do get it, the happiness doesn't last, and finally, the pursuit itself causes dissatisfaction during the longer time between the happy moments of getting things. We stress ourselves in the search, and when we stop that, it feels good—and we call that happiness.

This is not unlike the cycles of mental-emotional abuse in some partnerships. If someone gradually abuses you over time, and they suddenly stop the abuse or even treat you nice, you will feel relief, perhaps happy, and even grateful (and that may even be called love). This does not mean the stress in between is healthy, natural, or acceptable. We will stop abusing ourselves when we come to realize the pursuit is futile and that actually, we need nothing in order to be happy.

You Need Nothing to Be Happy

You may have practical reasons to have things, but don't pursue things *for* happiness. You don't need a single thing to be happy.

Happiness is your natural inner state, when you are not frustrating yourself about acquiring or keeping things.

Happiness based on needing worldly things is short-lived and vulnerable; it is at the mercy of a sideways look, a job loss, or a stomach pain. It is a momentary rest, a short gap between two sorrows.

True happiness is not vulnerable because it does not depend on circumstances. It has no cause, and what has no cause is immovable. It cannot disappear for lack of stimulation. It is not something gained; it is a state of freedom from sorrow.

Happiness cannot be lost, but once believed lost due to some cause, it cannot be known, and you can be lost in looking for it where it is not.

As revered mystic Papaji said, "You don't need something to be happy. You need something to be unhappy." Some "thing" like a thought about wanting or needing something or someone, or a bad thought-feeling about something or someone, which you believe and savor.

Wanting is the Cause of Unhappiness

It is because you're unhappy that you want to be happy. Find out the truth about why you're unhappy; find out what you want. That want is invariably based on false knowledge of what you think you have to have. That lie and the truth will be revealed when you switch your state. What I discovered is that we can feel good and be happy now, without what we want. You will learn how later in this book.

Positive Thinking Makes You Miserable

Many people are beginning to recognize that happiness is not in things. There have been attempts to look within, but we have been immersed so deeply in false beliefs, and are surrounded by a majority that is still submerged, that people are flailing and struggling.

Perhaps we first tried to use thought to feel better because it has been so dominant, with most people's lives lived out of their heads. The positive thinking movement was at least a little warmer, looking a bit closer to the source. But positive thinking is also still pursuing some "thing" that will "make" you happy. Yet, how well does it work? Are you free? Or are you dependent on unreliable thought?

Have you ever tried to force a positive thought on a bad feeling? If you've ever tried really hard, then you know how frustrating and painful it can be. That's because you are trying to do the impossible, to mentally convince yourself of something while every cell in your body is screaming, "No, that's not true!" You believe a strong feeling while trying to believe a flimsy thought.

The desire for happiness is not a problem; the right use of the body-mind is intensely pleasant and there's nothing wrong with feeling good. It is the search for object-happiness, as a temporary fix for unhappiness, which is the problem.

Denial, Deletion, and Distortion

Positive thinking can be a form of denial, deletion, or even distortion. We cannot feel one way and think another—that is being incongruent, and we simply cannot accept incongruence;

it is not functional. If some fact or truth comes to light that is not in agreement or alignment with your belief, it threatens your very sense of reality. You will be agitated and restless and this conflict will not be allowed to remain that way; the situation must be reconciled for harmony to be restored, somehow.

We will do one of three things 1) repress, deny, or ignore the truth, 2) twist and distort thoughts about reality (but the truth never goes away, nor does the agitation), or 3) we change our beliefs. If there's one thing we must have, it's congruency (at least in our minds, if not with truth).

Thoughts *about* experience or actions can be anything; they can be easily twisted and distorted and have nothing to do with fact, reality, or truth. For example, say someone at work says, "You cut your hair." In your mind that can become distorted into, "She hates my hair," or "She loves my hair," and then you experience one or the other. Are you experiencing what happened, are you experiencing what is true? No. You are experiencing your thoughts *about* what happened. You deleted what was actually said. The truth is a co-worker noticed your hair was cut.

The thought "Nobody can hurt me unless I let them," is both denial and distortion, a mental attempt to reconcile pain (pain caused by believing that someone hurt you), with the thought that it's not possible for them to hurt you. Which do you want, the thought or the actuality? This claim allows you to have the thought "no-one can hurt you," yet keeps you in pain and illusory bondage to others.

Almost all of the time, our mind reads that someone is trying to hurt us are not true. Even if it is true that someone's intention is to hurt you, they still can't and don't do the hurting. Only you can. It is your thought, which you believe, *about* their actions or words that hurts you, *never* their actual words or actions, (short of physical violence). Let them have their intent; it can only harm them, not you, and you can't do anything about it anyway.

Accepting a distortion is a lazy and poor option; it can be a very painful and confusing position, and more so as time goes on because it does not actually work for you; it is not freedom and peace. Many mental conditions are littered with distortions and delusions. It is much healthier to look at what's actually going on, and accept it. Either it is true that nobody can hurt you, or it is not true. This is called integrity.

Sticks and Stones May Break My Bones

—but names will never hurt me! This childhood mantra served me well (internally, never outwardly, because I did not want to give the bullies the idea they should use sticks and stones). I clearly saw the truth in it. These days, with rampant bullying, there are many people saying that words and name calling do hurt. Their intention is good, to protect bullied children, and it is a call to action to address this serious issue.

Yet are we really doing children a favor by teaching that names can hurt us? We'd be better off going to the root, teaching that our believed thoughts *about* what others say is what actually hurts us, and teaching children to discern the difference. When we stop hurting ourselves, when we stop acting like names can hurt us, mental bullies will no longer exist.

Physical Pain Does Not Cause Unhappiness

You can be in physical pain, and laugh wholeheartedly, as I am sure you know. In physical injury, added mental-emotional pain can be worse than the physical, and is completely unnecessary.

For example, some parents think that young children who bite can be taught how it hurts by biting them back to show them. Whether or not this makes sense or works, I don't know.

But one parent who was bit savagely hard knew that he bit back in anger, and he did not want to do that. There is correction, and there is over-correction. Any action taken out of reaction to emotional pain is over-correction. Upon close scrutiny in an *Alchemy* session, he discovered it was not the bodily pain that hurt the most. The accompanying thought "You are going to hurt me - I am going to hurt you back!" is what caused the emotional up-rise.

What was buried in the moment was the belief that the child's intention was to hurt him. But every attack is a cry for help. People are hurting, wanting, and lashing out the only way they have known how, either due to childish immaturity, or ignorance. Yet people always have a positive driving intention for every such action, for themselves if not others, (although that may not be obvious looking just at behavior). The child was unhappy, her state was agitated, and she wanted something. Instead of paying attention to that, we can narrow attention to our judgmental thoughts about her behavior, and neglect the ecology of the whole situation, and the child.

This embodied realization enabled the parent to have better understanding and compassion for the child, as well as access to the wisdom of other possible resourceful actions, and freedom to apply them.

Physical pain is not a cause of unhappiness. Deeply submerged in mental-emotional pain, we can even neglect the physical problem. In the case of physical injury, what is needed is to stop the outer cause. With mental-emotional injury, we must stop the inside cause. Sometimes you need to do both; just don't confuse one for the other.

Why Do People Stress to Be Happy?

Why have people been pursuing things and trying to control or distort their thoughts if these strategies have never worked, and even caused more pain? It's almost like an illness that everyone has, and so therefore no one knows. Yet it's also glaringly obvious.

Perhaps the mentally ill or the ones that break down and crash are like the canaries in the coal mine, the first to "fall" in a toxic environment. (Canaries were brought into early coal mines as a warning system for invisible but deadly gas buildup. A dead canary meant it was evacuation time.) These people could be our early warning signs, pointing to a fundamental problem which we have been ignoring, and so the problem grows.

There is no one single cause for how this state of affairs came to be in society. A myriad of things contribute to our current condition: I have mentioned movies, news, marketing, etc., but those are just the means by which the message is perpetuated.

To our credit, we have done our best with what we have, and we have not known what else to do. The originating factor is lack of awareness and false knowledge; because, to paraphrase Abraham Maslow: when all you have is a hammer, everything looks like a nail. All we've ever thought or believed is that things, people, or events make us happy, so that is where we look, that is where we apply ourselves.

Additionally, there is the phenomena known as "the majority rules," (which can also be called mass unconsciousness); generally, people do not want to be different from others, so they do not question the status quo. They do not question the happiness belief.

Turn Around, You Are Not Bound

Well it's time to disregard society, to challenge it, and to stop looking for all the "why's" you hurt, because you can, and because you are needed if we are to leap beyond society's painfully attached and even dangerous position. Our technological skills, science, and weapons have far surpassed our mental-emotional skills and development. It's time to drop the childish attachments and catch up.

When you are peaceful within, your outer actions and behaviors are peaceful. When individuals are peaceful, communities are peaceful. When communities are peaceful, cities are peaceful. When cities are peaceful, countries are peaceful. When countries are peaceful, the world is peaceful. There is no world peace without your inner peace. Inner peace comes before outer peace. That is how important you are.

To discover inner peace, a full understanding of the "happiness paradox," is needed so that we can stop living backwards.

Chapter 5

The Happiness Paradox

The Process of Living Backwards

The "why's" are where the suffering lies.

What happens when you notice a good feeling? Do you attribute it to something you just saw, heard, or remembered? What happens when you notice a bad feeling? Do you become aware of persons, places, things, or events around you, and look for a cause? If you don't see one in your immediate experience do you wonder, "Why do I feel bad?" and then proceed to think about it until you find a painful thought that fits? "Ah yes, that's why I feel bad, "X" happened, or is going to happen." In this way, we live in the non-existent past, or the imaginary future.

Imaginary Living

The potent irony is that mind is always after the fact. One day while washing the floor, I knocked the bucket and a lot of water splashed up and over the pail, covering the floor. Moments later, mind said, "There's water on the floor." I burst out laughing because I already knew that. I did not need a redundant thought to tell me that. Mind always comes in after circumstances or events, and makes claims, judgments, and conclusions (about the past or the future), as if thought were true. Worry and fear are exactly that; mind either reliving the past, or fearfully concocting the future, neither of which are happening now. Either way, it's all unreal, it's all imaginary.

Engaged, absorbed, and lost in the past pain or future worry that mind presents, by the time a bad feeling has grown big enough so that we notice it, often a myriad of thoughts and beliefs have already been accepted, consciously or below conscious awareness. While you are fearing the past and worrying about the future, you are doing it now. Is this the best use of your now?

While I encourage you to not live in the mental past or future, this is not accomplished by controlling thoughts.

Thoughts are Not a Problem

The brain is a mighty reflex organ and database, and one thought, image, taste, touch, or scent leads to another. You cannot "control" thoughts; if you could you'd know what thought is coming next, and you'd never have a thought you didn't want.

While you cannot control thoughts, you can chose not to believe them, not to entertain them, and to not put your attention on them. Thoughts are like birds, the more you feed them, the more they will come, and when you stop feeding them, they stop coming so much. As well, when you clear the confusion of false beliefs and directly see truth, painful thoughts fall away on their own.

False Proof Causes Confusion

Believing you need some thing or someone, you go around agitating yourself until you get it. It's much like hitting your thumb with a hammer—oh how good it feels when you stop!

In the same way, you decide you have to have something or someone, you agitate yourself, and then if you get it, you stop agitating yourself and you feel better. In this way, you confuse the good feeling with the object or person, attributing it to them—and so you repeat and start feeling bad with the next wanting. Pleasure follows pain in a never-ending cycle, so even getting what you want is pain, in the big picture. You are a mouse on a wheel, perpetually running after satisfaction and peace, which can never be reached in your predicament. There is an easier way; you can just quit banging yourself.

As long as human behavior is dominated by desire and fear there is not much hope for humanity. In our society most people are moved by the endless pain-pleasure cycle. Actions springing from confusion and pain result in more confusion and pain for yourself and others. As the mystic Sri Nisargadatta Maharaj said, "Circumstances and conditions rule the ignorant; the wise is not compelled, the only law he obeys is that of love."

The Rabbit-Killing Tree

Because we are not aware of what is going on in our body-mind, when we switch from knowing love to knowing "love lost," or "love denied," we miss the truth that we and only we are the cause and source of how we feel. It's a confusion that is illustrated by the ancient eastern story, "The Rabbit-Killing Tree."

It goes something like this: A hunter and his dog walk through the woods and unwittingly scare a rabbit out of the brush. The rabbit darts out and runs smack dab into a tree, falling dead. That night, while enjoying rabbit stew, the hunter contemplates the rabbit-killing tree, and instead of hunting the next day, he returns to sit and wait by the tree. He waits all day, but it doesn't produce one rabbit, so he goes home hungry.

Like the hunter, we have been confused and mistaken people, things, and events for feeling, and there are two reasons our beliefs appears to be true.

The primary one is because you are the authority in your experience. What you accept, say, and believe with integrity, you will experience. It's your life according to you.

The secondary reason is that our beliefs are not original; we have accepted the beliefs of others as our own, unquestioned, and not watched closely enough to discover the actual truth.

Not only have we suffered needlessly due to this ignorance, we also have not known our full potential; the mind-boggling capacity of the body-mind for cosmic experiences of love and joy.

The False Hierarchy of Happiness

Believing that things make us happy, we have placed a happiness value on things, and therefore created a hierarchy of happiness: ice cream comes with a certain level of happiness, compared to a new relationship, which comes with a different level of happiness that we allow ourselves to have.

This was never as glaringly obvious to me as a couple years ago when I saw the biggest sign in my life, screaming: "Bigger Toy, Bigger Joy!" It was a car dealership.

I thought of all the people that year who would see that sign, believe it to be true, and who would not be able to afford a new car, and thus be left with less joy, because they believe it. People struggling with poverty have been known to suffer severely at Christmas time, and to even do criminal things in order to "bring home" the joy.

Close to the car on the false hierarchy of joy is an intimate partner. Satisfied with the love and joy of a conventional and happy relationship, once established in one, people think that's as good as it gets. I've had married friends enthusiastically wish me the happiness of the love they have found. But 'other-love' is a tiny expression of the love we are capable of knowing. *It has to be*, due to the very nature of putting all our love into one small part of vast existence. Perhaps in seeking universal love, we grab the highest item on our hierarchy, and thus infinite love becomes mistaken for one person.

In that mistake, love has been reduced, minimized and limited. Real love is not just love for one; it embraces all equally and is therefore infinitely larger. To me, my friends' exaltation of "other" love is like holding a candle to the sun and exclaiming, "The candle is the greatest light there is!"

So while I appreciate the good intention, I chuckle inside, and privately wish them the discovery of the infinite, eternal treasure within. (Don't mistake me, it's not that one should not have a partner; it is the confusion of the source of love that blinds and binds you, causing attached suffering, putting you at the risk of loss of love, and limiting your joy.)

The trap is this: As long as you are pleased with lesser desires and pleasures, you cannot have the highest. Whatever pleases you holds you back, and is transient, bound to leave, change, die, or become unsatisfactory eventually anyway.

Many people, famous and ordinary, have acquired everything materially possible, money, a partner, family, etc., and still they were unhappy. Some suffered severely enough to commit suicide. Some, like Eckart Tolle and Byron Katie, escaped suicide and discovered the true source.

Happiness has not and never will be found in things, people, or events. What do you gain, having attached yourself to the impermanent world, as you miss the real, infinite source? You run on the material-world-wheel, chasing the next "thing," never being satisfied. What you lose is knowing your own ever-present freedom, peace, and bliss.

The more strongly you believe you need some object or person, the more you try to control the outside, and the more you try to control the outside, the more frustrated you become because it's not possible. The longer you live, or the harder you try, eventually you will realize you cannot control things. Why waste a whole lifetime? Inevitably, you will be denied, and it could be one of the greatest things to ever happen to you.

The Gift of Being Denied What You Want

Through being told and sold in countless ways that others can hurt us or make us happy, we blindly accepted these thoughts as true. It is not until we are denied what we want that we have the opportunity to actually test the validity of our belief; otherwise we continue running on the wheel in ignorance. However, being denied does not mean that we necessarily *will* test the thoughts.

We could just as well engage in suffering based on inherited beliefs, and in an attempt to feel better we may tell ourselves ugly things about others, digging ourselves deeper into pain and ignorance. That option means we don't have to question our model of reality and we can mentally stay congruent within the illusion. So being denied what you want is to be offered an opportunity and choice: ignorance and suffering, or truth and freedom.

To Be Happy, Quit Trying to Be Happy

Beyond the false beliefs that you use to make yourself unhappy, it is actually the very thought, "I want to be happy, (and I need 'X')," that makes you unhappy. *Wanting hurts*. It is dissatisfaction itself. Making happiness dependent on something outside your control, something impermanent, some "thing" somewhere out in the future, and not here and now—is suffering.

I know that at first not wanting things in order to be happy goes against the grain, *but it's a false grain*. It only looks like a paradox because we didn't know better (because our parents didn't know better, or theirs). We were not aware enough to see what was actually going on, we've been living backwards by seeking happiness in all the wrong places, and we've been living out of our minds, living through false beliefs by opting for those beliefs—even over the truth of our own experience.

Here are just a few examples of that:

1 - You can notice a good feeling, but deny it because you "should not" feel good because A, B or C has happened. I experienced this about a month and a half after Dad died. Out of the blue I noticed a good feeling arise, and as crazy as it sounds, I believed the next thought, which was, "But Dad died, I can't feel good." Another month later when it happened again, the thought, "Could I be happy?" arose, and gradually, I let myself feel the natural happiness and peace that never left me; I was the one who had abandoned it.

2 - The source of love has only ever been experienced within us, yet we have attributed it to others, placing impossible demands on them. No one can make you happy; it is not within their power. So you set them up for failure, then demand happiness from them. Thus, current romantic notions and needs of love are actually acts of violence.

3 - Everything changes, but we can mentally try to control things to keep them from changing. A rose is precious because it is temporary. If a rose's scent never left, all there would be is the scent of a rose, and so *there'd be no scent*. Change is fundamental to experience, without it, there'd be no experience.

4 – You have a thought about someone, and the truth is that you have no way of knowing if it is true for them. But still you proclaim it to be true, to yourself or others. This is arrogance, and violence. Who are you to dictate what is true for another? Through these mind reads, you limit others in your mind (and in their mind, if they hear and believe you), and you limit your experience and relationship with them.

5 - We suffer over death as if it is not part of life, and believe we must mourn, and for a long time. We have confused mourning for love, as if you can't have one without the other. We also believe death is a bad thing, yet we have absolutely nothing to base this on, in truth.

It All Adds Up

While chasing momentary objective pleasure, we agitate ourselves, missing the inherent joy of now. The happiness of acquisition is a mental one, and the happiness of the mind comes and goes as easily as thoughts do. So we ride the waves of ups and downs, much like an addict does.

Our minds have been filled with the false so that we're blinded and ignorant to truth, causing confusion and incongruence with reality, which we've denied or distorted. On top of it all, we have limited our joy. No wonder people are struggling!

But if you clean up the false knowledge, you will allow joy beyond belief to shine through.

Chapter 6

Joy Beyond Belief

We don't want things, people, or events.
We want the feeling we mistake them for.
You can have it any time.

Initially, my ambitions were just to seek relief by moving my attention from what I mentally did not want, onto what I did want. After a while of keeping it there one day, I noticed that it started to feel good. So I kept attention there, and the longer I cultivated the good feeling that way, the greater it grew, until one day floodgates of gratitude opened and overcame me.

Having no object that "caused" this, I realized I could know and experience it any time, any place, and without reason or cause. So I began to experiment with it, knowing and growing joyful experiences, with gratitude. One day, in the middle of what I call a "Feel Good Fest," the thought arose "Oh, you can't feel *that* good," along with inner agreement because, "Nothing has happened to give me it," and with increasing speed, the fabulous feeling took a speedy nose-dive.

It is said that two swords cannot fit into one sheath. It is the same with feeling; you can only feel either good or bad in any one moment. I saw it all happen, and so switched back to the good feeling. It was then that I knew, without doubt, that the thought we believe—meaning the thought we put and keep our attention on—is the one we experience. How simple. How direct. How obvious.

Since things, people, or events have nothing to do with our happiness, we are free, and our happiness is unlimited. You are capable of much more joy than you have lived—or imagined! In fact, it has been your imagination that has limited you.

I began ignoring old thoughts and beliefs that would limit or curtail the joy, and began experiencing more and more, and higher and higher blissful states…for no reason. For weeks I went around in a happy, joyful, even excited state no matter what I was doing. Eventually somewhat tired, I also discovered that peace and calm were additional flavors available to me. That was a good thing, because one cannot be in a blissful state all the time; the body does need rest.

My Unshakable Discoveries

In my own direct experience, I discovered:

- Immediate relief from stress.
- Pleasure and heights of blissful joy that I did not know were even possible, and for absolutely no reason.
- That what I experience is dependent upon what I accept to be true, and nothing and no one else.
- What causes my pain is believing thoughts *about* people, things, or events.
- Acknowledgement and acceptance of this truth and of my power of authority to chose.

Over about nine months the bliss leveled out into a peaceful, contented equanimity that has not left, even though I went through poverty and bill collector calls, being rear-ended in car accidents, a herniated disc, a friend's sudden passing of cancer, the surprise death of my other father, and more. Even though I knew my old beliefs would have had me suffering, all I ever felt, and feel, is love and compassion. (Note they are not beliefs).

Since discovering and sharing joy, I have been privileged to witness people drop the lie and transform, through truth, right before my eyes!

You don't need to believe in anything to have this experience or know the unshakable truth. Everyone can shift state, transcend problems, and heal without having to control thoughts or heal the past, because it's in the power of now that you are already perfect and healthy.

To make the shift and feel good, first you have to deserve happiness.

Chapter 7

How to Deserve Happiness

To deserve happiness, stand in your integrity and:

1. Don't expect or want it to be "given" from anything or anyone.
2. Have no interest in the "whys" that you hurt, or in what others do or don't do.
3. Value inner happiness above all else including the material, objective world.
4. Reject any desire for the outside; it is a trap. Look only within for what you want.
5. Be interested in feeling good, first and foremost. Make it your priority.
6. Know happiness is already available; seek it in faith.

People have mistaken their self value for entitlement to happiness, and have mistaken happiness for things, and so anger or resentment may arise when they are denied worldly things. But happiness and your innate value are not the same.

As long as you do the opposite of these six things (which most of us have been taught to do), lasting happiness and peace are impossible. All of this is free to you; nothing else is needed to deserve happiness. Until you make use of it, you do not deserve it. Only those who are truly, earnestly, interested in happiness and value it as the highest deserve it; only they will attain it.

Ready to feel good in five minutes?

Chapter 8

How to Feel Good in Five Minutes

Use Your Three Powers

Both "good" feeling and "bad" feeling use the same nervous system. The same energy running through the body-mind can be used to feel good or to feel bad, and the nervous system is very fast. All that is needed to switch tracks is a flip of attention. In fact, you don't even need five minutes to begin feeling better; it starts instantly.

Use your power of awareness to know that you are feeling bad (and that you are putting your attention on a bad thought), then use your power of interest (in feeling good) to put your power of attention on what you *do* want, and keep it there. Energy flows where attention goes, and the longer you stay with what you do want, the better you will feel. More detailed instructions on this come in the next chapter.

Yes, you can feel better and even good in five minutes, but if you have attachments, the feeling won't last long, and problems will keep arising in what may appear to be patterns. The pattern is pointing to the same attachment. You need to learn how to stay with the direct grounding of the body to ride through the waves of the mind long enough to shift state and have a breakthrough that dissolves the attachment once and for all. This is easier than it sounds, because thought is actually powerless.

Monkey Mind is Powerless

The function of suffering and happiness is simple. What's complicated is the 'monkey mind,' which due to the freedom of imagination, can spew out *anything* that often has nothing whatsoever to truth, and is often something painful due to bad-feeling beliefs, or even simply out of pure habit.

Mind is faster than the nervous system, faster than feeling, and quickly offers up habitual thoughts and beliefs, but remember, thoughts only arise as *options* for you to put your interest in and attention on, not necessities. Thought, or mind, is like the moon; it has no power source of its own, it merely reflects the light of the sun. You are the sun.

Mind derives its power from you, and the next chapter will show you how to simply use your authority and integrity to pull the plug whenever you want, so that you can use mind instead of it seemingly using you.

Chapter 9

Seven Steps to Lasting Happiness and Inner Peace

What do you do when you come to recognize that your hand-me-down beliefs have never fit, and never will? Being ready now, how can you break through and actualize joy beyond belief, for no reason? The very same way I did.

1. Recognize Truth

Recognize the truth that the cause of your pain and your happiness is within, and only within. This is critical to your freedom, happiness, and peace.

2. Stand in Your Integrity

If you have seen the truth of the cause of pain and happiness once, know that if it's true in one situation, it's true in all situations. You "know it intellectually" to be true? Good enough. Act accordingly, and like riding a bike, it may be awkward at first, but you will come to effortlessly embody it.

3. Move from Blame to Claim

Refuse to blame the outside in any way. Not with your actions, nor through words, thoughts, or energy. Claim the source to be within, without blaming yourself either. This will leave space for a new experience, and a new expression of your being that stems from love.

4. Come to Your Senses

Like your breathing, you can take conscious control of your power of attention. If you do not take control of attention, it is still there. It just goes on autopilot, wandering, and it can wander where you don't want it to go. I'll demonstrate.

As you read this right now, can you feel your left foot? Yes, now that I have mentioned it? What happened, had your foot stopped feeling? No, that can't be, right? You focused your power of attention onto my words, or your thoughts about my words. That is how powerful you are; so powerful you can actually eliminate a body part from your experience.

How much more easily can you eliminate knowledge and wisdom? When you focus your power of attention on one thing, you eliminate practically everything else. This is what happens in what we call a "blind rage." Effectively, you become blind, deaf, and ignorant not only to people and things around you, but to your very own body, which can be held hostage in a bad state, all tense and knotted up.

Feel your foot again, and then your right shoulder. Did you notice the movement when going from the foot to the shoulder? If not, play around with it right now until you do. That sensation of movement is due to attention being narrowed.

As children, we were taught to focus and narrow attention, particularly when reading. Yet, as you read this, can you be aware of your peripheral vision (seeing things around you) at the same time? Yes you can, right?

So you can also open your power of attention. Now take a moment to open attention and feel your feet *at the same time* as the top of your head. This should be easy. If it is not, it is because you are narrowing attention and moving it back and forth, trying to narrow it in both places at once, which is not possible, so you will experience it as stressful or tiring. Just relax, be still, and open.

Now, feeling your feet and the top of your head at the same time, and looking softly straight ahead, taking in your peripheral vision, also notice your breath moving in, and out, all at the same time. Do this for a few in and out breaths.

~

What do you notice? How does it feel? Quiet? Calm? Still? Empty? Peaceful? Relaxed? Spacious? It feels quiet and calm because you are withdrawing the power of your attention from the stream of thinking. I call this practice "coming to your senses."

Accustomed to living life as if all there is is thought, some people *think* about feeling at first. So they think thoughts, and then say they don't feel anything. But feeling is done with the body, not a thought. Ignore thoughts for a while, be silent, and feel into the body.

Some people say they notice "nothing." Of course, with the body alive that is not possible, but if you have lived years of your life in your head, you have primarily known only thought, and when you come to your senses there is little or no thought, and so it can initially seem like "nothing." But just stay with it and you will begin to notice things you had not noticed before, like the noise of the fan, the light, the fridge, little noises from outdoors, tension in the body, maybe even your heartbeat. Whatever you notice, use it to bring attention back into the senses: the feet, the head, the peripheral vision, and the breath. This is a relaxed, open, unattached, and therefore more intelligent state that you can now use.

5. Question Every Bad Thought-Feeling

When you make feeling good your highest priority, even more important than what's going on around you, then you quickly notice when you feel bad in any way. When you notice a bad feeling, don't accept it—*suspect it!* Use it as your guide, to know when your attention has moved in the wrong direction and that you need to shift state so that you can see things more clearly. Doing so will turn your perspective and world around; villains will become victims, and compassion will kick in.

Every bad thought-feeling arises because there is attachment of some sort. You want something, or you don't want something. Either way, you want something. Use the noticing of a bad feeling to practice *Alchemy* by asking yourself the first question:

What Do I Want?

Answer this question like a child. If I took a toy away from a child who began to cry, and then asked her what she wanted, the answer would be "I want the toy!" Very simple, very direct, very honest, and very clearly the opposite of what is not wanted (which is the toy taken away).

Your answer will feel like relief at first, and it must feel complete and pure, leaving no bad taste. It should be a thing, person, or event (not a feeling), and it must be stated in the positive.

Do not judge what you want, or deny yourself for any reason. Do not try to be "bigger" than it, or to "transcend" the desire in any way. Just admit it. A child would not say, "I just want to be free and at peace without the toy." Be brutally honest with yourself. It does not matter what the answer is because the second question will handle it.

If you are having trouble identifying what you want, verbalize what you don't want, and turn it around. Once you know what you DO want, ask yourself the second question.

How Does It Feel?

Be certain to ask and answer in the present tense. You are not asking how it would feel "if" you had or didn't have something. That would still be attachment, still believing you need it, still confusing it with feeling. (Note that the feeling and the object are not the same things.)

You are simply asking how having it *does* feel, so that you can access the feeling, now. You do know how it feels, otherwise there would be no sense of a problem. In order to know the problem, you must know the solution.

Now you are putting your attention on the solution feeling, not the problem feeling.

6. Shift Your State

Since we feel with the body, not a thought, to shift your state you must not merely think about how it feels. Get the mental answers to what you want first, then come to your senses and ask, "How does it feel?" again, but this time ask your *body* for the answer to how it feels; look into the body for the answer as a feeling. When you make contact with how what you want feels, spend some time enjoying it, exploring it, and appreciating it.

From this open, better-feeling state, you will have access to information and intelligence that you did not have from the bad-feeling state. It is from this state that people have major "Aha" breakthroughs, outbursts of the laughter of realization, and what they mentally know to be true becomes embodied. Body and mind come into alignment.

A clean, strong, good feeling shift will alter your experience, perspective, and your response to things, people, and events, and realizations and learnings may flow from it. You may get a big enough, "OH! Aha," which signals the complete and final destruction of the perceived problem. That problem will never arise again; you are free. Bondage is having problems; they attention, take time, effort, and energy.

During those ah-has, people often realize that what they thought happened to them actually never did. This is the ultimate in forgiveness: realizing there was never was anything to forgive in the first place, and then you are also forgiven.

In working with people, I am always looking for that 360 degree flip, and encouraging people not to settle, but to go after it, rather than merely using *Alchemy* as a temporary feel good band-aid. You need a good strong state to be able to face the attachment fully and uproot it, cleaning it all up inside.

Use the Other Five Questions

Sometimes you do not get the "Big OH!" which is utterly transforming and often results in uproarious laughter, with just the first two questions. There are seven questions in the practice of *Alchemy*. The first two *Alchemy* questions shift your state, and from there the remaining five go after the attachment and the "Big OH!" Learn all seven *Alchemy* questions to free yourself from all attachments, so that inner peace may prevail. You can download the cheat sheet free here: http://InnerAlcove/cheat-sheet/

7. Get a Practice Partner

At first, because you are so used to following the slippery slope of the mind, it is best to work with someone who can help facilitate your shift. This is critical if you are not successful on your own at first.

That person's job is to ask you the questions, and to notice when you have not answered the questions positively, or when you have begun to follow a train of thinking that does not feel good and/or does not answer the question. In this way, they help you keep attention on what you do want, not what you don't want.

They will be your mirror, until you enter the age of integrity.

Chapter 10

The Age of Integrity

As long as we all keep thinking things or people or events make us happy or unhappy, we will personally struggle with money, work, health, and relationships, and we will raise the next generation the same way, instilling fear from infancy.

In order for us to make the next leap forward, we must realize that thoughts are not who we are, realize the truth about pain and joy, and live with integrity and in congruency with those truths—with body, speech and mind aligned.

> "Embody what you teach,
> and teach only what you have embodied."
> ~ Dan Millman, The Way of the Peaceful Warrior

This will be an age of true love. Instead of fearing or needing others, it will be a time of taking responsibility, without blaming oneself. It will also be the end of confusion.

Because it takes no time to stand in your authority, the age of integrity that leads to a social leap in consciousness could be a very short one, for you, but either way, it is a necessary stage.

Whether you see it or not, whether you like it or not, whether you accept it or not, as the authority in your life, you are the only cause of your pain and happiness. That is simply how the body-mind functions. The sooner that is seen, the sooner the pain and confusion will end, revealing your ever-present, natural, joyful birthright. Before society quits lying, we must quit lying to ourselves. For this, we can turn to the only useful fairy tale we were ever told.

Chapter 11

Pinocchio Points the Way

Integrity is Irreplaceable

Perhaps the only true fairy tale we were ever told was Pinocchio. Basically, the message was that if you lie, something bad is going to happen. Pinocchio taught us integrity. He could not have integrity just some of the time, for the more little tales he told, the longer his nose grew, and the more obvious his lies became.

For integrity you need awareness and willingness to look closely to discern true knowledge before accepting something as true. The statement, "Oh, I know nobody can hurt me, *unless I let them,*" signals the growing pains of a society that is trying to grow up, yet not quite ready to fully abandon the false security of old, painful, untrue beliefs. But partial abandonment is not abandonment, and it won't work.

"Nobody can hurt me, unless I let them," sounds a little better than, "He hurt me," but what this actually means has not been thought through. Let's take a close look: what is this "letting" that you are doing? What are they actually doing that hurts you? Whatever it is, apparently they are still the one hurting you. So the first part: "Nobody can hurt me," is completely negated by the second part. This thought is rubbish.

"Free yourself. Don't wait for us."
~ Byron Katie, Author of *Loving What Is*

Knowledge vs. Wisdom

In one of my favorite movies, "Peaceful Warrior," the teacher (Socrates, Nick Nolte) says, "Knowledge is knowing what to do, wisdom is doing it."

This degree of integrity applies to speech also. Any parrot can utter the sounds, "I know I am the cause of my pain," but does he truly comprehend and therefore embody, experience, and live it? No. Parroting is not intelligence.

"I know that intellectually..." is a lament common to people I work with, and they trail off, grasping for words to complete it, often with something like "...but I need to 'get it in my cells,' permanently." There is a sense that there must be more, that something is missing, that something is off.

I knew it intellectually too, and I wanted final, fundamental, 360 degree reversal of my experience and behavior. Love was the driving energy. I wanted to act on what I knew, with integrity, and to know love, and give only love.

Because we can tend to worship thought over the rest of reality, the mental difference between knowing and doing may seem subtle, but the gap between knowing a thought and accepting it as truth so it can be experienced and embodied, can be a chasm. Hopefully you notice, with dissatisfaction, the incongruity of knowing vs. doing, and find it unacceptable, which keeps you seeking a satisfactory solution.

The solution is integrity; it is the bridge between the knowing and being. Embodying the truth that I knew mentally was something that I loved and desired, and therefore moved towards. But when people say it to me, it is an objection, a mental reason to not accept the truth. "I won't believe it until I have it in my cells," is what they are saying. But you won't have it in your cells until you truly accept and believe it; until you stand up for it, until you act on it.

You Are the Authority

The reason (excuse) we give for suffering is what creates it. If you believe (for any reason you believe) that you should feel bad, then you do. You will experience the bad thought-feeling that you believe. I call them thought-feelings because in our experience they arise together and are inseparable. Having convinced yourself that things make you happy or unhappy, you are bound by your conviction. For better or worse, you are the authority, and I can prove it.

The Speech Experiment

As an experiment, think of a time when you felt bad. Stop and think about the situation, and notice one of the bad thoughts around it.

Then ask yourself, "Who told you to say that?" Is there anybody else is in there, telling you what to think, believe, and say? Nobody, right? It's just you.

Since You are the Authority
—What are You Waiting For?

When you feel bad, as long as you believe that something or someone outside of you caused it, you will blame them, and you will suffer that blame.

Alternatively, knowing that the cause is within you, you will turn inward, where the pain is, and look to see what is actually hurting you. You will notice the thoughts you are believing, thoughts which you have brought to life in your experience by narrowing and focusing all of your power of attention onto them. You will see how you are hurting yourself in this way, and only then can you stop.

You can free yourself in that moment, and when you do, and you look back, you can see that what you thought to be true was not. Now you are detached from object or other need. You are free, and happiness is not obscured, so it is restored.

I've had hundreds of sessions like this with people, where their pain turns to laughter (you can listen to some here: http://InnerAlcove.com/laughter). Many clients have had these experiences multiple times, and yet still, somehow people can say, "I know it mentally," but I need to, "get it in my cells." I am giving you a heads-up on this very common, apparent, yet illusory road block. Don't believe it.

If you believe that you need to "get it in your cells," then that is what your experience will be, and you will continue to blame others. How will you know when it is "in your cells" anyway? As long as you hold this conceptual need and thought to be true over your actual experience, then you will never get it in your cells.

What proof do you need in order for you to say that you know things, people, or events are not what cause your pain? How many times do you need to have this proof? If you hold onto your integrity, all you need is once, and then you won't need any more time. You will never mentally or verbally blame things, people, or events again.

Otherwise, you will *always* need time to "get it in your cells" because what you say and believe goes.

Don't Trust Thought

Your brain's job is to offer up thoughts as options, not truth. And it does a magnificent job of that, spinning out thousands of thoughts a day. Many of them are simply habitual. You don't believe them all. What you do believe effectively becomes your truth, your experience.

Until we stand in our integrity and accept the consequences of what we choose to believe, until we stop believing mere thoughts simply because they arise, we are forever bound. So don't trust thought.

Don't Trust Feelings

If you want permanent knowing and to live and embody what you know with conviction, then don't trust feelings, because by their very nature, feelings come and go.

Does knowing the truth that you are the one hurting yourself mean you will never feel bad? No. And if you did feel bad, does that mean you don't have the knowing "in your cells?" No. If you believe that, then it would again be you unwittingly being the authority and blaming it on something outside you, on a feeling. Feeling is impermanent and is not wisdom or knowledge—it is a known, not knowing itself. Don't use feeling to dictate what you know.

Even cells come and go; where you need it is not "in your cells." That is just a conceptual thought. Since thoughts and feelings are transient, unstable, and unreliable, *what can you trust?*

The Problem is the Solution

You have heard and learned a lot of thought-knowledge in your life, but you don't remember it all, don't believe it all, don't repeat it all, and you don't embody it all. Knowingly or unwittingly, you have chosen some thought-knowledge over others.

Thoughts and feelings also come and go, but in order for change to be known, it must happen against some unchanging background; it must be witnessed. You are the witness, and as such you do not come and go, and that permanence is your power of authority.

You are the authority, and that is only a problem when you don't know it. You don't know it when you are believing that something else is the cause, or when you believe something else is needed; when you are narrowing your interest and attention onto outside things, events, or thoughts, being absorbed in them, and losing yourself in them. In this way, you abandon your integrity and authority.

Because you are the authority, you are the problem; but because you are the authority, you are also the solution.

Uphold Truth, No Matter What

Once you have seen the truth of what causes pain, you must uphold the truth, never blaming the outside again. That is how knowing the truth of the cause of your pain and joy is permanent in you, as you. Once you know something, you can never not know it.

Until you have seen the truth, or when wavering even after having seen it, have faith in your thought-knowledge, and try truth on, cling to it as you push and test it as far as you can take it. That is the way to break through your own self-inflicted catch-22 of demanding proof; because until you do, you will not have proof.

Like I did, refuse to blame. Otherwise, you will never say, once and for all, "Yes, it is true, nobody hurts me, I do," and you will continue living a painful life of illusion in ignorance, as if people can hurt you. As Henry Ford once said, "Whether you think you can or whether you think you can't, you're right." You are the only authority in your life, and you are very powerful, *but only if you know it*. If you don't know it, you are in trouble.

As the authority, there's only one thing left to do; get out of your own way.

Chapter 12

Get Out of Your Way

Unless you get out of your own way, you are like a beggar who all his life doesn't know he's sitting on a bucket of gold. Well, actually, now you know, so in this case you'd be like a beggar who refuses to look in the bucket.

I've heard many excuses for not stepping into your authority and not discovering the true source of happiness:

Minimization: "My life is not that bad."
Well, I didn't think mine was either, mostly. I didn't know how attached and at risk I was until my attachment was torn away from me, excruciatingly. And I didn't know how limited I was. Sometimes we do need pain to wake us up and get us moving in the right direction (but then its job is done and it is no longer needed). The "my life is not that bad" rationale is like owning a Ferrari and never driving it faster than ten miles an hour, or buying a rocket and never launching it.

Laziness: "It's too hard."
How hard is it to suffer? If it takes you fifteen minutes, thirty minutes, or an hour to shift your state (which it usually does not), is that better than a day of suffering? A week of suffering? A month? A lifetime of suffering?

Resistance: "Do I have to watch everything I think?"
No, just notice how you feel, good or bad. That will let you know when you are attached.

Disbelief: "It's too simple, it can't be true."
Alchemy is powerful *because* it is simple, easy to remember, can be done anywhere, anytime. It is simple because truth is simple. What's complicated is the mind, and *Alchemy* bypasses it.

The Past: "I've been too damaged from the past."
Alchemy does not use the past, because feeling is here now. All there is, is now. So it doesn't matter what has happened to you in the past. I've worked with people who have been disfigured from accidents in the past, abused as children in the past, raped in the past, and had depression in the past, and all were able to shift.

Resignation: "I've tried everything, nothing works."
Alchemy is unlike anything you've seen, and in fact, it goes against much of what we've been taught. Almost everything out there requires something outside of you to change, like thoughts, circumstances, atmospheres, people, or jobs. Or requires a "healing" or a healer of some sort. This makes you dependent and keeps you bound. Some programs will help you "manage stress." Not end it, not free you. Or other things are vague or conceptual. *Alchemy* is actual and direct; provable in your own experience.

Discomfort: "I don't like talking about feelings."
Well good, you don't have to, and actually, you should not. Feelings are thoughts, and there are hundreds of them (mostly bad). The power of *Alchemy* is in feeling, not thoughts. It is very simple; there are really only two ways you are feeling, either

good or bad. We work with simply knowing which you are feeling at any time.

Specialness: "My situation is different."
While circumstances or events vary, the mechanism of suffering is the same for all, no matter what. The circumstances or events themselves don't actually ever hurt us; our believed thought-feelings about them do. Therefore you can end mental-emotional suffering.

Medical: "I'm on medication."
That's okay, do the practice and get to the psychological root. Sometimes physical medication is needed for a while; *Alchemy* complements your treatment.

Perceived pain value: "We need pain, it motivates us to change."
Has change ever happened while you were feeling good? We do not have to feel bad to change, as I am sure you know from your own life experiences. Actually, feeling bad more often *demotivates* than motivates. Using *Alchemy*, pain can be used, when noticed, to wake you up and move you toward a better feeling.

Healing the past: "Don't we need to go into the past to get messages or "lessons" in order to heal?"
What does "to heal" mean? Does it mean to feel good now and stay with the present joy that is only available here, now? Does "healing" mean to get or receive learning or understanding?

Our learning and understanding can only come from taking on a different, wider perspective, now. Suffering is by nature a very narrow perspective. An open, wide perspective comes with feeling better (and vice versa). Feeling better is done now, and learning comes now. So-called "going into the past" only replays suffering, re-living it now. It narrows the now and will bring little or no understanding.

Additionally, there isn't any such thing as the past. It is just your memory of the past; and that's just a thought, mental image, or sound, played now. Don't let a memory of the past be your identity in the present.

Beyond getting lessons, you are whole and healed when you stop thinking that you are not, and that does not need time or the past. In fact, it requires that you stop dredging up the past to suffer-over now. If something you cling to from the past is repeating in your present, use *Alchemy* in the now, in this present moment, where the power is.

Not special enough: "You are somehow special and I am not." Again, the structure of suffering is the same for everyone; through not knowing any better, I suffered the same. It was not the suffering that brought me joy; that's impossible. It was the joy. I had decided I'd had enough, and that is all you need too.

Karma: "It's my karma, I have no choice but to suffer in this life." Well, who told you to say that? Remember: You chose; you are the authority of what you believe and therefore experience.

Since you are here reading, maybe it was your karma to get this book, to hear this message, and to discover what is possible.

Embarrassment: "I am embarrassed to be struggling, and find it hard to ask for help."

Still, how embarrassing is your behavior right now? You may have withdrawn and kept to yourself. But that does not go unnoticed either.

How honorable is it to want to overcome generations of wrong and painful conditioned beliefs? Beliefs that have resulted in atrocities, war and mass murders…? Remember, inner peace comes before outer peace – that is how important you are.

Distrust: "I don't believe you."
Good, don't believe me. This is not about belief, and you only ever believe yourself anyway. That is how it is for everyone. You are on your own; you must discover for yourself.

There is one common denominator in all these objections; you. Once again, you are the authority of your experience—and you don't even realize it. You believe an excuse by being interested in it, putting your attention on it, and then becoming absorbed and involved in the content, *and you miss that you do that*. That is the biggest and only true problem.

Whatever "but" you put in your way, is yours. Get your "but" out of your face, stop thinking about it, and just do it and see what actually happens.

Remember, because you can get so invisibly in your own way, at first you may need someone to act as a facilitator to help you breakthrough, so you can blow-out the belief that has held you captive all your life.

Chapter 13

Blow-out the Belief that Has Held you Captive all Your Life

—the belief that anything outside of you makes you happy or unhappy

Even that belief has not held you captive; you have held it. When you see, in your own experience, that it is not true that things hurt you or make you happy, in order to stay congruent, you will do one of three things. You will deny, rationalize, or minimize the experience, twist or distort the truth through thought, or you will drop the belief.

The latter is exactly what happened to me. There I was, faced with joy in the middle of circumstances which I and the rest of the world would agree were "good reasons" to suffer. Every time I put my attention on those reasons, I hurt, and every time I put my attention on the love, joy and peace, I felt good. There was a lot of flip-flopping at first, because both cannot be held at once, so I had to let go of one or the other.

Since I came to a point of "no more" pain, zero tolerance, and since the joy was such an immense relief, I denied the painful thoughts by staying with the joy.

Doing so was such a huge contrast and undeniable shift that the learning was not limited to what happened in that specific incident; it generalized out into realizing this was true in all instances of mental-emotional pain. I quit stressing out about all the things I used to think I had to stress about. The truth was undeniable; nothing, no-thing, is depressing or painful, except a bad thought-feeling, which you can access and imagine any time. That covers all problems you have, with all people; there is no problem with other that is not self.

You don't need a reason to be happy, and even with reason to be unhappy (like a bad thought), you can be happy. Face adversity feeling good, and you too will blow out the false belief, and find freedom. There are seven challenges before you, but one single solution.

Chapter 14

The Seven Challenges (or Opportunities)

In our current condition, happiness and peace of mind are hard to attain for these reasons:

1. You were taught, in countless ways, that your happiness depends on something or someone else,
2. You have strong unconscious beliefs of which you're not even aware (e.g. that things make you happy/unhappy, that how good you feel is dictated by the thing, etc.),
3. You may have established a low level of happiness as your norm, or a high level of suffering tolerance,
4. You have become very good at knowing what you *don't* want, so good that it's easy to access and…
5. You may not know what you *do* want,
6. Being so absorbed with mind (and what you don't want), you may be out of practice with how what you do want feels, or even with feeling itself and,
7. Everyone else around you believes and speaks as if things, people, and events make us happy or unhappy, and there's pressure to conform.

With the majority of people believing that things, people, and events "make" us happy or unhappy, it is especially important at first to find a friend who no longer believes the lie, or who at least knows it "intellectually." Share this book and your new learnings with an old friend, or make a new one. You can join the Inner Alcove, an online course and a supportive community of people learning to work with attention with the common goal of mastery and inner peace and freedom. Practitioners support each other as well as get assistance from myself and other Facilitators. Visit: http://InnerAlcove.com

The Single Solution

The good news is that when you shift your inner state without any change in outer circumstances, you are effectively proving Challenge #1 wrong, you uproot unconscious beliefs (#2), you raise your level of happiness (#3), you drop what you don't want (#4), you become better at knowing what you do want (#5), you take energy away from the stream of negative thinking and begin to recognize feeling, and it gets easier to access good feeling (#6). You do not feel the need to suffer any more, even if others do, and compassion, the wish that someone not suffer, is awakened for others.

The best way to end someone else's suffering is to end your own. So you stop feeding and supporting even the mildest mental-emotional suffering; you are no longer contributing to society's current condition (#7).

All of that can happen from simply shifting your state using your powers of awareness, interest, and attention.

The Final Question

The most important question is, *are you ready?* How much pain do you need? What is the cost of that stress to your body, friends, family, finances, work, and play? *Have you had enough?*

When working with people, after they make the shift and breakthrough, they sometimes experience regret over their past bad behavior, which they now understand never needed to happen. They can start to think about how many years they feel they've wasted, and how many relationships that didn't need to suffer.

Of course, then I help them with that form of suffering too, but the message here is *don't wait any longer*. You don't have to put up with pain one minute more.

The only thing you need is the sincere and earnest desire for do-it-yourself happiness that needs nothing.

Chapter 15

Do-It-Yourself (DIY) Happiness

As you know by now, *all* of your experience is actually do-it-yourself (DIY), the good, the bad, and the ugly. Even if you think something or someone is making you happy, it's still DIY—you are doing it, even if you are not aware of it, or don't know how you are doing it. After all, "He makes me so happy," is but a thought, a mere comment, which comes *after* the happiness that already is.

If you are to fully realize and actualize the true source and cause of feeling, you need to stand in your authority, recognize the truth of experience, and claim your DIY happiness.

The Truth Experiment

As an experiment now, just touch one hand with the other, feeling skin and bone. You know how that feels right? Okay, now feel it with love. You know how love feels, right?

~

Notice the difference? You might even notice a smile. It feels different, but it's the same hand. Now, did anything outside of you change? Did anything or anyone "give" you love? Where *is* the love? What *is* the source? Not in another person, right?

Simply by coming to your senses, feeling into the body, and looking for happiness, you will find it—any time. So, *seek joy!* Give it to you yourself wherever you are, whether you are alone or with someone. Do it driving the car, doing groceries, cleaning the toilet; wherever and whenever. It's like riding a bike, the more you do it, the easier it gets. I challenge you to raise the bar and live life feeling better and better.

This experiment also demonstrates your power of interest. When your interest is in feeling skin and bones, that is what you get. When your interest is in feeling love, that is what you get.

When you notice a good, happy, or peaceful feeling, instead of believing it's the puppy, or the child, or the car, or the partner, instead of looking around for the outer reason "why" you are happy (which is just a mental narrowing), come to your senses, turn within, and put your attention on the very source of happiness, and hold it there, appreciating, and enjoying the feeling. Acknowledge its presence here. You'll be surprised at what may happen. What do you have to lose anyway…except some painful, old, limiting beliefs that have never served you, and never will.

Next: Happiness is not the only thing that is DIY.

Chapter 16

Do-It-Yourself (DIY) Love

Tainted Love or True Love?

Yes, even love is DIY. Have you ever felt disconnected from someone you love? How did you act? Distant? Uninterested? Disconnected, right? What were you waiting for? For the person to do something, so you could feel connected? What if it did not happen? Then would you feel hurt? Ignored? Angry?

There was a belief that they had to do or say something before you could feel connected, before you could give the loving connection that you demanded from them, right? Make a note of this: The love you withhold is the pain you feel. They are not the cause of your feeling of disconnection. You are.

What if you could feel connected first? How would you act then? Connected? Caring? Loving? How much more likely is that to get you the (outer) connection that you want? Give yourself everything you've been denying, and then some! Become so full of love that no one can hurt you, and you cannot hurt anyone. Know yourself as the whole and complete being you are. This is how to be the change you want to see.

You Don't Need Someone's Love

After weeks of happiness, bliss, and peace, one morning I woke with a dream in memory, and noticed a feeling that was not my new norm, not joyful. I dreamt of someone who I'd like in my life (but who was not) giving attention to someone else. Immediately I began to practice.

"What do I want?"

Hmmm…this took a moment or two as the dream fog began to clear…And then it came:

"I want to feel that person's love."

"How does that person's love feel?"

As I reached for the feeling wonderful images, smiles, and loving memories flashed; and a warm, tingly sensation began to flow through my body.

"Is this what I prefer to feel?"

"Yessssssss, hehe."

"Who's love did I need?"

"Ohhh mine, and I am so grateful that it is here for me!"

"Feeling this way, how do I act?"

I reflected on the dream again, and this time enjoyed the other's enjoyment, happiness, and interaction with the other person. There were no negative feelings of loss or jealousy (that may have been what they were, although I never gave them my time or attention long enough to label them), there was just infinite love. The pleasure grew as a smile stretched across my face.

"Is this what I prefer to do, give, or send?"

Definitely—I wanted to know, give, or experience love, and project love for that person, even in their absence. As I continued to enjoy those sensations, the overall feeling of love grew, expanded, and enveloped me. I snuggled deeper into the pillows and sheets with pleasure, and my body warmed as if glowing.

The love got better and better, and at the peak I was shocked to recognized that this feeling was *exactly* what it felt like when that person was here, "giving" (I thought, at the time) love "to me." A realization was re-affirmed, and it anchored in:

I was the source of the feeling then, when they were here,
just as I am the source of it now, when they are not!

The cause was not the other person then, as it was not now. Even the very sense of other comes from within you, whether they are present or not. It is felt in your body-mind. Thinking about that; how could it be any other way? A playful giggle arose, followed closely by laughter. The cosmic joke is so much fun. Who's love did I need? Mine. It was my love that I have only ever had or wanted.

Oh yes, and what of that bad feeling I awoke with? Long gone and long forgotten! Lingering longer in bed, I savored the love, and then bliss bloomed from a yet larger expansion: there was no more subject or object of love; it was just pure love.

Enjoy your self—Self is all *you ever do enjoy!*

Popping the Bubble

Since pain and joy reside within you, you can use the *Alchemy* questions for any and all suffering, including the absence of a loved one. In that case, the second question would be, "How does having him here feel?" Beginners sometimes object with, "But it's not real, it's not the same, he's not here, it's just imaginary." Actually it's the other way around: it's been imaginary that he was the source of your joy.

The "it's not real" response exposes ignorance of truth and confusion of persons, things, or events with feeling. The question was not "Is he here," (which yes, would not be true to say he is), but "How does having him here feel?"

Furthermore, when you say it's not real and therefore you can't feel it - Who's telling you to say that? Who's the authority? You are. And you are limiting your love and joy based on your chosen imaginary belief.

Finally, and as I am sure you've experienced, you can be right beside someone and feel utterly alone just as much as you can be beside them and feel love. So what does the person matter? If they were the source and cause of love, as long as they were with you, you'd *never* feel alone.

Love Before You Think™

Our society pitches the need to find the perfect partner, which means you have needs and wants that the partner must meet; it pitches attachment love, which is doomed from the start. Two people needing and demanding things from each other is not love, it is trading.

Having learned the painful pitfalls to this form of relating, you can see the importance of not seeking the perfect partner, but to seek to see with perfect eyes.

When you are self-fulfilling, you can freely love your partner without need, and the partnership works better. When you think you need your partner to do something in order for you to feel loved, respected, accepted, or good in any way, before you can love naturally, then *you* are not being loving. You are all in your head, and thinking before loving.

Use *Alchemy* to shift your state from need to love. In other words, *love before you think* (and certainly before you act or speak), and you will see things in a new light; your thoughts and understanding will be clear and compassionate. You will actually see and experience the other person, not just your narrow, needy or fearful thoughts. The light of awareness will shine wisdom on the totality of the situation, the other person, and yourself. Apparent problems will dissolve and not even need addressing.

Love Before You Think™ is a program for partners in the Inner Alcove where individuals first learn to love before they think, and then to hold space for each other to enable clear seeing, freedom, and peace.

Love before you think—it creates a safe space where personal masks can drop so that true intimacy and unlimited love can be known, through innocence.

Chapter 17

The End is a Return to Innocence

Innocence is Bliss

You don't need thoughts, for *anything*. You don't need a thought to walk, or eat, or sleep. You don't need a thought about the future (the future will become the now without that). Knowing a thought about the future is not knowledge of the future, it's merely knowing a thought now. You don't need any of it to live and function now.

Needing nothing to be happy and needing a thought, some "knowledge," to be unhappy illustrates how "Innocence is bliss" is true! Knowledge is stress, and not knowing is the end of stress. The following story illustrates the problem that knowledge presents.

Is it a Snake, or a Rope?

In bygone days, a merchant who for years would not take a particular shorter trail because there was a snake on it. One day he traveled with a wise companion, who said "Come, let's take this path; there is no snake." At first the merchant refused, but his friend drew him in for a closer look. "See – *it's a coiled rope.*" Suddenly the merchant could see the truth that had always been the case, that indeed there was no snake.

Nothing real blocks you from knowing all the answers to your childhood questions; it's just that false knowledge stands in your way. Trying to learn truth is useless when the mind is blind to the false, by the false. You will just learn more false concepts. This is why we must question everything we think we know afresh, with the innocent eyes of a child.

Knowledge Pollutes

Say you discover a paradise island, and staking your claim, you mark off your land. When you are done drawing the border, you think you have proclaimed what is yours, but what you have really done is proclaimed what is *not* yours! Which is greater, what you lose, or gain?

Even holding knowledge of a good belief (e.g. "I am a kind person.") is a limit. Beliefs may work for you for a while, but they are like boats. On a journey you may need a boat to take you across the river, but in order to continue on your journey, you must abandon the boat. Use beliefs, but don't cling to them, lest you get stuck.

You cannot know perfection; only imperfection can be known. Knowledge, by its very nature, is narrowing and limiting. For knowledge to be, lines must be drawn, labels proclaimed, and borders, boundaries, and divisions made, where there actually are none. In practicality, we need some of these to communicate, however it is the personal mental-emotional clinging to thought knowledge that causes separation, disharmony, and suffering.

Say you dislike another person, and you believe ugly things about them. These thoughts do not hurt the other, but they do bother you. Before those thoughts, there is happiness and peace. As Byron Katie asks: "Who would you be, if you could not think that thought?" The only way to know perfection is to reject knowledge.

Not Knowing is Knowing Truth

We never truly know anything to be true; what you think you know is just a thought. You are knowing a mere thought, be it pleasant or painful. Let's put thought in its proper place, as the bodily function and tool that it is, not as who or what you are, and not as truth.

To Know Truth, Don't Lie

There is one Earth, and seven billion people, with nearly all of them living in their own illusory world of mental constructs, mostly painful. So there are nearly seven billion dream worlds, in conflict with each other. When you become real and end your own inner illusory conflict, you end numberless conflicts of others too, in a ripple effect.

Pinocchio wanted to be a real boy. To do that, he had to stop lying. For you to end your illusion and know truth and lasting happiness, you must stop believing the false, and you must stop lying, to yourself and to others. Look closely, see a thought as just a thought, stop believing bad thoughts, stop blaming. Question your conditioning, and guard your speech with integrity. Speak only what you know as actual truth (not mere concept), act only on what is true, and in this way you drop the illusion, leave space for truth, illuminate truth, and bring body, speech, and mind into alignment with truth.

This may sound like a lot, but in fact it is simple and easy when you seek joy. Simply only be interested in what you *do* want, not what you don't want. Use suffering for the only thing it is good for—to point you towards joy.

Only then can you know the truth about where and what your source of pain is. Only then can you be finally happy. You were born a bundle of innocent joy, and to reclaim joy, simply drop knowledge and return to the innocence of not knowing. You will begin living forwards, unleashing your true potential.

Looking directly within, peel away every attachment until you reach a happiness ratio that starts with zero. Peel the onion until you reach the final root of all fears; the existential fear, the idea of a tiny self, apparently born to grow old, suffer, and die. Then peel that away too. Until all the layers have been peeled away, you will not know the truth about the ultimate lie, that of the personal fairy tale.

The Personal Fairy Tale

After Dad passed away and I walked through the hospital walls, stunned, I made him a promise that "it would not be for nothing;" meaning his suffering, our family's suffering, and my suffering, the whole event, would not be for nothing. I did not know how, or exactly what that meant, but I was determined find out.

At first I thought it had to do with abundance, because Dad struggled financially. Later I realized that poverty was a symptom, not a cause. What I really wanted to do, I realized, was to find an end to suffering. As you recall, when I began my quest, I thought what I needed was to "control my state," no matter what was going on around me. What it turned out I was really seeking was detachment, so that there would be no need to try to control my state. That was only realized in retrospect. My desire for love and joy was what led me, willingly, to learn the truth about why and how we hurt or feel good.

The desire for things, people, or events—due to mistaking them for our happiness—stems from the fear of the ultimate fairy tale we've bought and sold; the one of personal separation. The fear of being a tiny, at-risk being in a massive universe means you must acquire, collect, and protect. The resulting liking and disliking, the stories and attitudes, are what we call character, and are collectively referred to as who we are: a person.

A person is just a bundle of stored memories and fears that trigger each other. Liking and disliking, habitual thoughts, and character are *acquired*, they arise from memory, and they are constantly changing.

You are not the effect of memory. Memory does not know you; memory is known *by* you. The body-mind you experience was born a blank slate. Memory, habit, and thoughts, are not original to you, they are not integral to you. They are not you. The idea of a personal self, with all its stories, and fears, and neuroses is narrow, and, well, selfish.

Alchemy begins to dismantle the personal, exposing it as the pain agent it is, and removing obstacles to the natural, expansive, joyful state. When you use *Alchemy* to shift your state, your perspective widens; it become ecological, whole with everything and everyone around you. You drop the narrow person you used to think you were. Abandoning the personal, you are no longer the limited individual; you are the universal. Then there is no fear, because who or what does the universal have to fear?

As the universal, and not the personal, there's no such thing as an, "old maid." You are free to be alone and happy, at any age. Whether or not you have a partner has nothing to do with your happiness, but in order to know and experience that truth, you have to see through the false lie, which you acquired from the generation before.

Yes, it is possible to know what is truly going on here, but what is necessary is to discard the false. There *are* people who know the answers to the existential questions at the beginning of this book, but not as thought—as direct, living truth. Return to child-like curiosity. Stop believing and start questioning what you think you know, and seek the company of people who do know truth. You will recognize them by not "getting" them; you will be confused, at least at first. That's a good thing, because when nothing is certain, everything is possible, and when something is certain, nothing else is possible.

A quiet, peaceful mind that does not know need, fear, or opinion is what is required for the ultimate truth about existence be known. First you must abandon desire and fear, abandon the personal. That does not mean to not acquire things, it means to stop seeking happiness and peace *in* what is acquired.

Freeing yourself from the pain of needs, wants, and attachment desires (in other words, your personal motives), you live a life that is so utterly different from what you now know. You come alive like never before; life is a fascinating moment-by-moment adventure, steeped in unlimited love and joy. Truly, by losing all, you gain everything.

Discarding all the personal stories, and then the personal fairy tale, without grasping, you reach joy without need, a state of non-attachment that comes with indescribable inner ease and freedom. That natural state is the absence of the personal, the absence of attached desire and fear. What is there, in the absence of desire or fear? All there is, is love.

May your return to purity, to the innocence of not knowing; to equanimity, joy, and peace, be swift.

Leave a Comment

http://TheHappinessLie.com

Buy Print Copies:

http://TheHappinessLie.com

Resources:

Join the Inner Alcove where you can meet real people and get supported in your discovery of lasting happiness and freedom: http://InnerAlcove.com

5 Biggest Mistakes People Make Trying to Be Happy Teleseminar: http://InnerPeaceTeleseminar.com

Witness the Laughter of Realization in this *Alchemy* Inner Peace Audio Program: http://InnerPeaceOfMind.com

Have an Inner Peace Discovery Session with Cindy http://InnerPeaceDiscovery.com

Get the Book, *Alchemy, How to Feel Good No Matter What:* http://AlchemyLoveJoy.com

About the Author

The simple and powerful practice of *Alchemy* came through her own suffering and later discovery of joy, and it emerged and took form in words, to help someone else.

Since then, her life has become happy and often ecstatic with the simplest of things. Filled with gratitude and unable to contain the joy, she was compelled to drop everything and write *Alchemy*.

Prior to that she was a print and web publisher and now she gives talks, facilitates retreats, gives private sessions, and operates the Inner Alcove, encouraging everyone to—*seek joy!*

Cindy resides in Ottawa, Canada.

More stories, her blog, and recordings can be accessed at:
http://AlchemyLoveJoy.com and
http://InnerAlcove.com

Made in the USA
San Bernardino, CA
24 June 2015